Little

Mermaid

Key sound er spellings: er, ear, ir, or, ur
Secondary sounds: ay, oi, sh

Written by Nick Page
Illustrated by Clare Fennell

Reading with phonics

How to use this book

The **Reading with phonics** series helps you to have fun with your child and to support their learning of phonics and reading. It is aimed at children who have learned the letter sounds and are building confidence in their reading.

Each title in the series focuses on a different key sound. The entertaining retelling of the story repeats this sound frequently, and the different spellings for the sound are highlighted in red type. The first activity at the back of the book provides practice in reading and using words that contain this sound. The key sound for **Little Mermaid** is er.

Start by reading the story to your child, asking them to join in with the refrain in bold. Next, encourage them to read the story with you. Give them a hand to decode tricky words.

Now look at the activity pages at the back of the book. These are intended for you and your child to enjoy together. Most are not activities to complete in pencil or pen, but by reading and talking or pointing.

The **Key sound** pages focus on one sound, and on the various different groups of letters that produce that sound. Encourage your child to read the different letter groups and complete the activity, so they become more aware of the variety of spellings there are for the same sound.

The **Letters together** pages look at three pairs or groups of letters and at the sounds they make as they work together. Help your child to read the words and trace the route on the word maps.

Rhyme is used a lot in these retellings. Whatever stage your child has reached in their learning of phonics, it is always good practice for them to listen carefully for sounds and find words that rhyme. The pages on **Rhyming words** take six words from the story and ask children to read and find other words that rhyme with them.

The **Sight words** pages focus on a number of sight words that occur regularly but can nonetheless be challenging. Many of these words are not sounded out following the rules of phonics and the easiest thing is for children to learn them by sight, so that they do not worry about decoding them. These pages encourage children to retell the story, practicing sight words as they do so.

The **Picture dictionary** page asks children to focus closely on nine words from the story. Encourage children to look carefully at each word, cover it with their hand, write it on a separate piece of paper, and finally, check it!

Do not complete all the activities at once – doing one each time you read will ensure that your child continues to enjoy the stories and the time you are spending together. **Have fun!**

Out in the ocean, deep under the sea,
lived a young mermaid called Coralie.
Swimming at dawn, one cold, early morn,
she heard a voice crying for help in the storm!

Little mermaid,
sing for me,
sing of the wonders
of under the sea!

There was Sir Bernard, perfect and brave,
hurled from his boat by a big, curly wave.
Coralie carried him back to the bay,
sang softly to wake him, and then swam away.

Little mermaid, sing for me,
sing of the wonders of under the sea!

Back in the palace, her head's in a whirl:
"Oh, how I wish that I was a real girl!"
Just then, a hermit crab said to the girlie,
"Why don't you call upon Seaweedy Shirley?"

Little mermaid, sing for me,
sing of the wonders of under the sea!

9

Shirley was purple and not very nice.
Her spells worked superbly but came at a price.
Nervously, Coralie swam through the ocean,
to see if this sea witch could give her a potion.

Little mermaid, sing for me,
sing of the wonders of under the sea!

Shirley said, "Certainly – give this a whirl.
Drink it. I promise you'll *be* a real girl.
Pay me by filling this shell with your voice!"
So Coralie paid – there was simply no choice.

Little mermaid, sing for me,
sing of the wonders of under the sea!

Drink it!

After her journey back, Coralie found
that now she had legs
right down to the ground.

When Bernard returned in his boat to the shore,
he said, "I'm quite certain I've met you before!"

Little mermaid, sing for me,
sing of the wonders of under the sea!

Coralie had no voice, not even a word,
but then something perfectly lovely occurred:
the boy held her closer, to offer a kiss . . .
and Seaweedy Shirley said, "I must stop this!"

Little mermaid, sing for me,
sing of the wonders of under the sea!

With Coralie's voice, she urged, "Come to me!"
And Bernard, enchanted, swerved into the sea!
Coralie stared but could not say a word.
Then, on a big rock, she spotted a bird.

Little mermaid, sing for me,
sing of the wonders of under the sea!

"Don't worry!" he said, "I know just what to do!
He pecked at the shell and he burst it in two.

Peck!

20

The curse was reversed, young Coralie learned.
She called out to Bernard – her voice
had returned!

Little mermaid, sing for me,
sing of the wonders of under the sea!

Seaweedy Shirley was chased far away,
and Coralie married Sir Bernard that day.

The mermaid's a girl –
she was granted her wish,
but sometimes she yearns
for the world of the fish!

Little mermaid, sing for me,
sing of the wonders of under the sea!

Key sound

There are several different groups of letters that make the **er** sound. Practice them by helping the mermaids sing some songs. Choose a tune and use a word from each shell in the first mermaid's song.

girl
whirl
bird
Sir
Shirley

curse
urge
curly
disturb
hurl
purple
return

Now do the same for the second and third mermaids. How many songs can you make?

nervous

Bernard

reverse

super

mermaid

swerve

word

worm

work

early

learn

pearl

Letters together

Look at these pairs of letters and say the sounds they make.

 ay oi sh

Follow the words that contain ay to help Sir Bernard get to the bay.

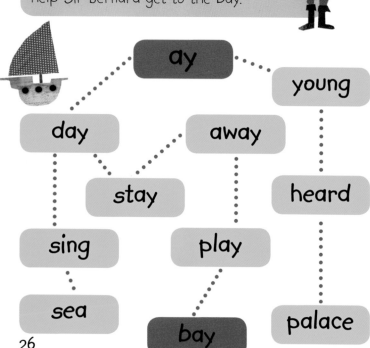

ay

young

day

away

stay

heard

sing

play

sea

bay

palace

Follow the words that contain oi to find Coralie's voice.

oi

choice

him

oil

boil

coins · · · · · point

hurl

noise · · · · · voice

give

Follow the words that contain sh to help the bird break the shell.

sh

show

shark

found

ship

sharp

word · · · · · stop

shell

Rhyming words

Read the words in the flowers and point to other words that rhyme with them.

	sea	
pea		tea
under		girl

	shell	
kiss		well
bell		word

	wave	
shell		brave
boat		cave

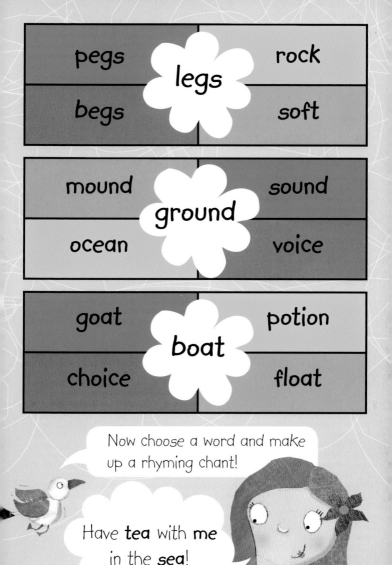

pegs	rock
legs	
begs	soft

mound	sound
ground	
ocean	voice

goat	potion
boat	
choice	float

Now choose a word and make up a rhyming chant!

Have **tea** with **me** in the **sea**!

Sight words

Many common words can be difficult to sound out. Practice them by reading these sentences about the story. Now make more sentences using other sight words from around the border.

Coralie lived **under** the sea.

The prince's **boat** was caught in a storm.

The shell broke and Coralie got **her** voice back.

Coralie and the prince **were** married.

her • see • me • suddenly • a

• they • are • just • from • one • were • then • them

When he heard Shirley, Bernard jumped into the sea.

Coralie told Shirley her **wish**.

Shirley **called** to the prince.

Coralie's voice was **inside** Shirley's shell.

Coralie's tail became **feet**.

The prince had seen Coralie **before**.

under • boat • sea • called • fish • feet • green • when • some • air • wish • birds

don't • before • he's • sun • wind • thing • inside • help

Picture dictionary

Look carefully at the pictures and the words.
Now cover the words, one at a time.
Can you remember how to write them?

bay

bird

boat

crab

fish

girl

mermaid

shell

wave